Space Coloring and Activity Book for Kids

By: Activity Nest
activitynest.org

This book is dedicated to the children of the world. May your hearts be full of joy.

If you enjoy the book, please consider leaving a review wherever you bought it.

ISBN: 978-1-951791-16-2

Copyright © 2019 by Activity Nest

ALL RIGHTS RESERVED

No part of this book may be reproduced, stored in a retrieval system, or transmitted in any form or by any means, electronic, mechanical, photocopying, recording, scanning, or otherwise, without the prior written permission of the publisher.

Get All Our New Releases For FREE!

Sign up to our VIP Newsletter to get all of our future releases absolutely free!

www.activitynest.org/free

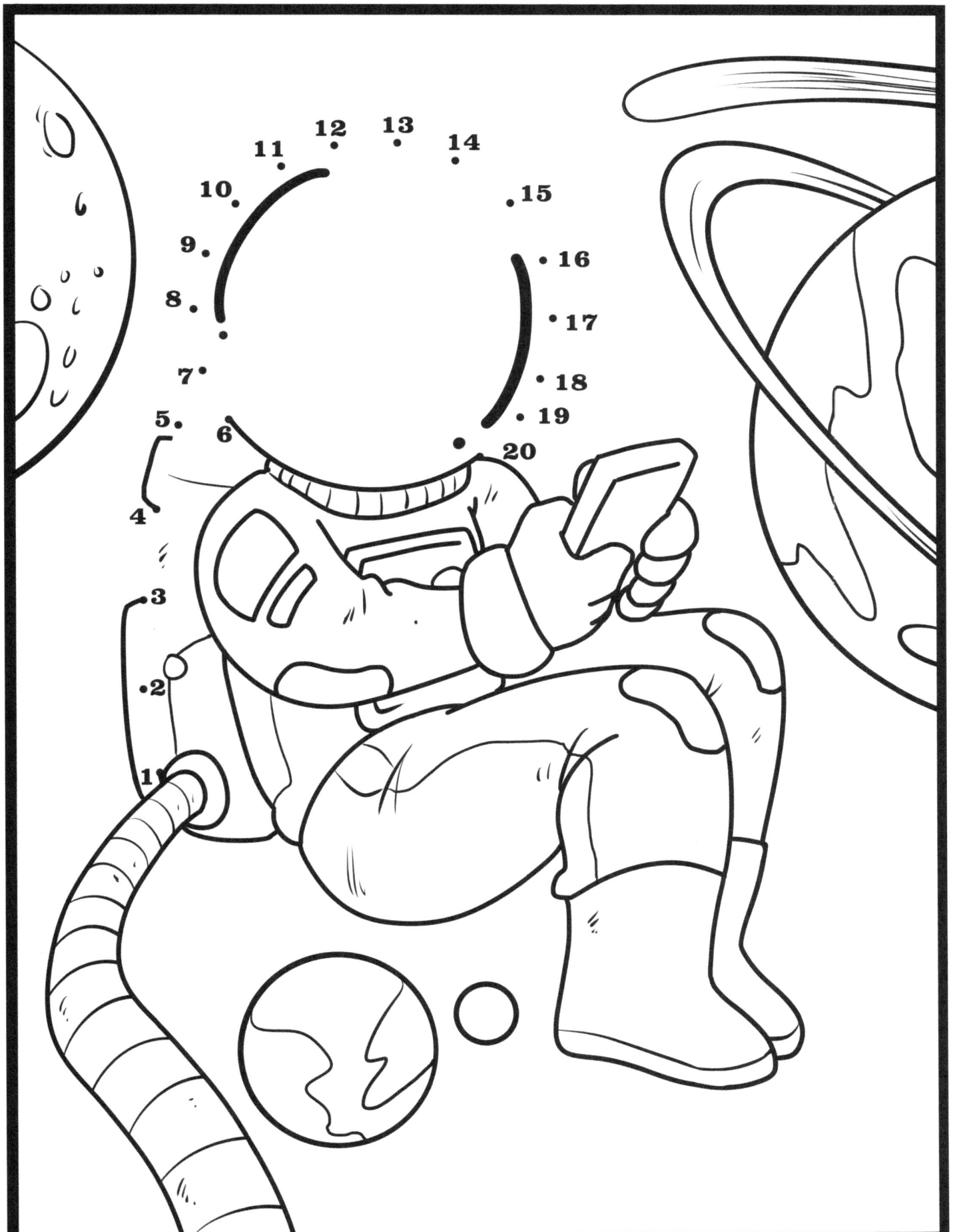

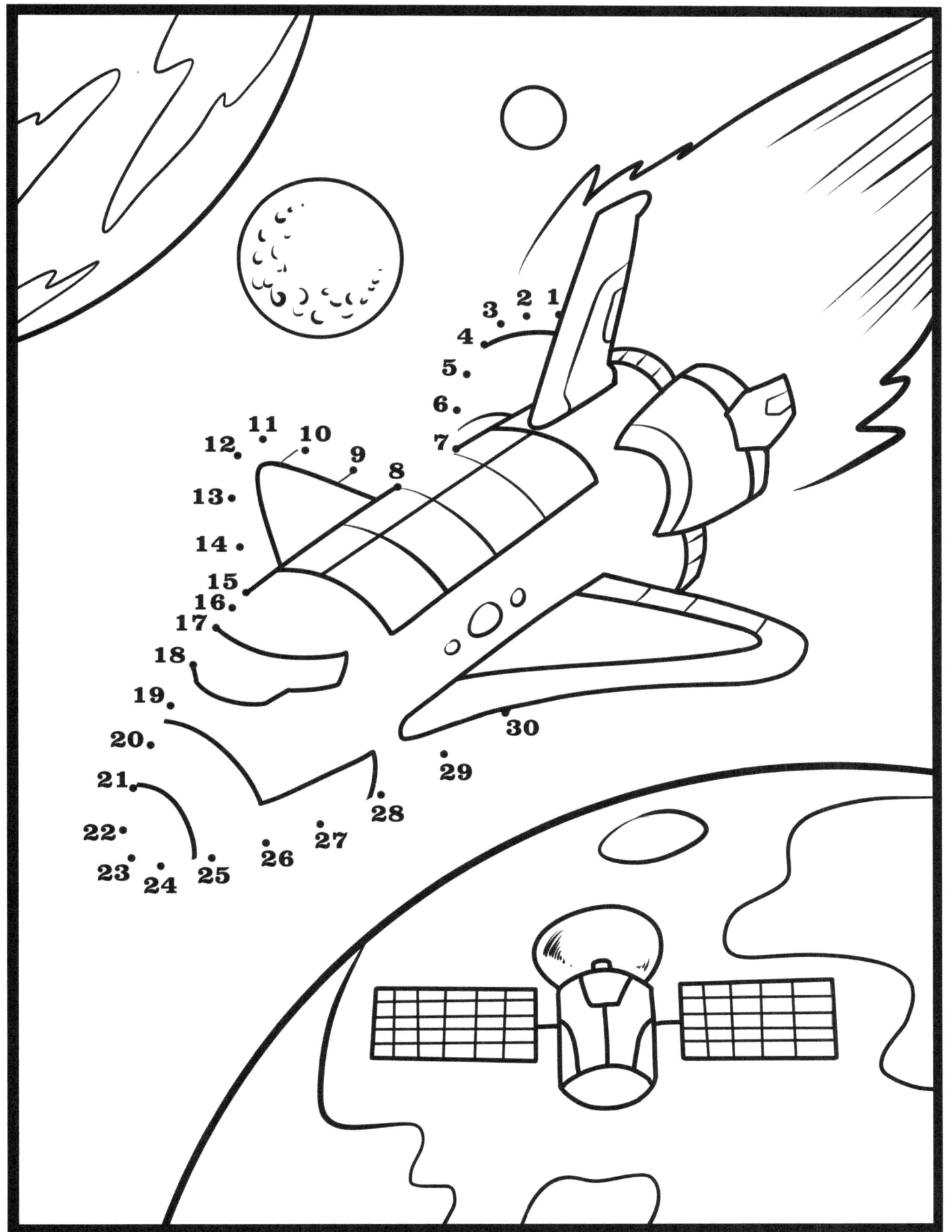

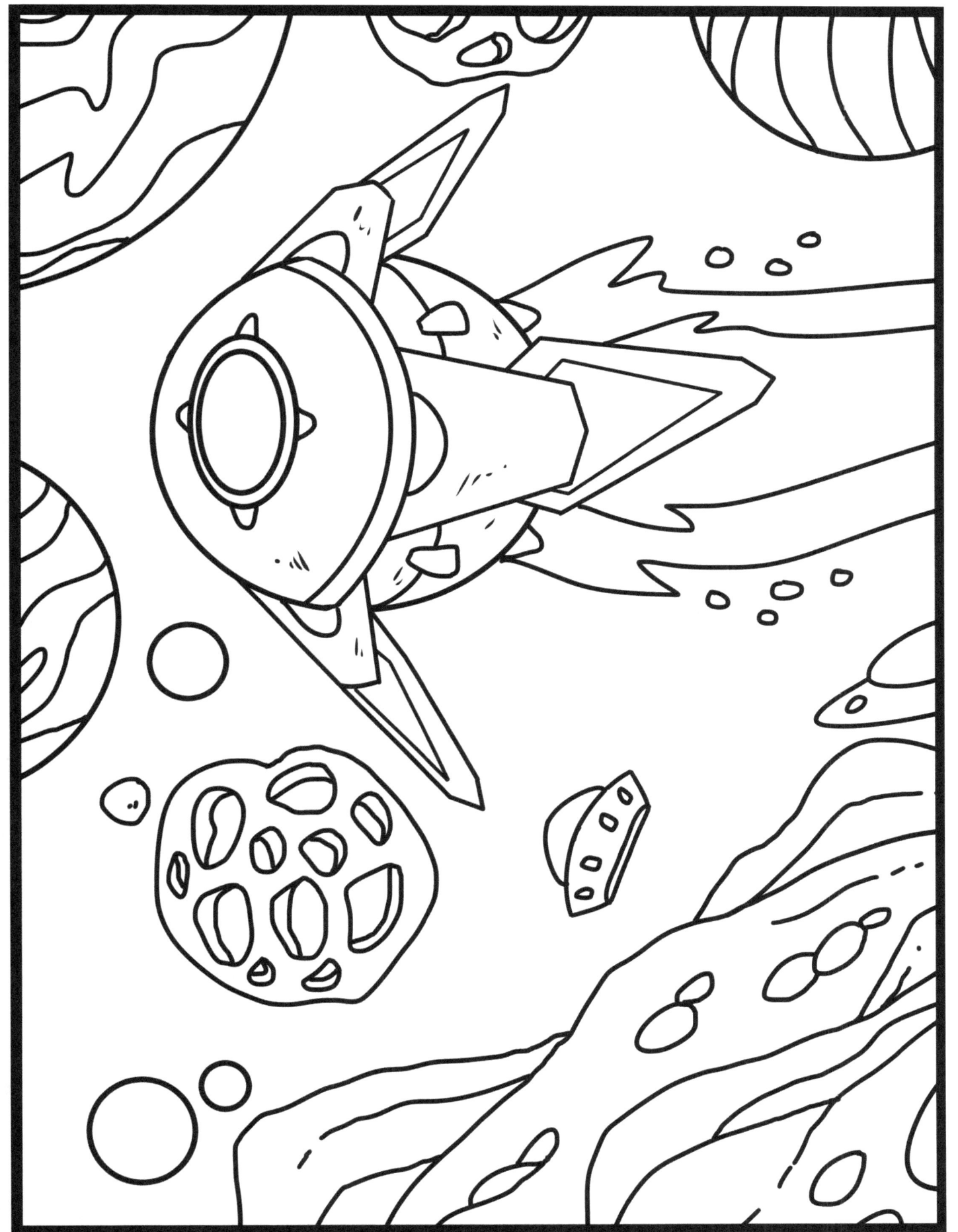

THANK YOU!
Please leave us a review on Amazon.

Amazon reviews are very important to our business and help other activity lovers find our books.

Please go to this book on Amazon and let us know your honest opinion.

It would mean the world to us. Thank you!

Don't forget to sign up to our VIP Newsletter to get all of our future releases absolutely free!

www.activitynest.org/free